US MILITARY FORCES

COAST GUARD

By Julia McDonnell

Gareth Stevens Publishing

Please visit our website, www.garethstevens.com. For a free color catalog of all our high-quality books, call toll free 1-800-542-2595 or fax 1-877-542-2596.

Library of Congress Cataloging-in-Publication Data

McDonnell, Julia, 1979-
Coast Guard / Julia McDonnell.
p. cm. — (US military forces)
Includes index.
ISBN 978-1-4339-5852-6 (pbk.)
ISBN 978-1-4339-5853-3 (6-pack)
ISBN 978-1-4339-5850-2 (library binding)
1. United States. Coast Guard—Juvenile literature. I. Title.
VG53.M38 2012
363.28'60973—dc22

2011000884

First Edition

Published in 2012 by
Gareth Stevens Publishing
111 East 14th Street, Suite 349
New York, NY 10003

Designer: Michael J. Flynn
Editor: Greg Roza

Photo credits: Cover, pp. 1, 17, 20 U.S. Coast Guard/Science Faction/Getty Images; p. 5 Chris Hondros/Getty Images; pp. 6, 9 Shutterstock.com; pp. 6–7 General Photographic Agency/Hulton Archive/Getty Images; p. 8 Mandel Ngan/AFP/Getty Images; p. 10 Rubberball/Frare Davis/Getty Images; pp. 11, 16, 21 U.S. Coast Guard/Getty Images; pp. 12, 13 Getty Images; pp. 14–15 iStockphoto.com; p. 18 Joyce Naltchayan/AFP/Getty Images; p. 19 Stocktrek Images/The Agency Collection/Getty Images; p. 22 Fotosearch/Archive Photos/Getty Images; p. 23 Hulton Archive/Getty Images; p. 24 Keith Meyers/AFP/Getty Images; pp. 24–25 Pool/AFP/Getty Images; p. 26 Wikimedia Commons; p. 27 Matt Stroshane/Getty Images; pp. 28, 29 uscg.mil.

Printed in the United States of America

CPSIA compliance information: Batch #CS11GS: For further information contact Gareth Stevens, New York, New York at 1-800-542-2595.

CONTENTS

Words in the glossary appear in **bold** type the first time they are used in the text.

THE NEED FOR A COAST GUARD

Every nation plans for the safety of its citizens. A military keeps a country's citizens and land secure during wartime. It also keeps a nation safe in times of peace, such as during natural **disasters** and accidents. Military forces may also protect citizens from people who break the law.

The smallest of our nation's five military branches does just what its name suggests: it guards US coasts and waterways and the people who live, play, and work on them. Although the US Coast Guard often serves alongside the other military branches around the world, its main responsibility is the nation's **maritime** needs at home.

What Are They Called?

"Coast guardsman" is the official name for any member of the coast guard—man or woman. The term "guardian" is also used. "Coastie" and "shipmate" are common nicknames. "Team Coast Guard" refers to the four types of coast guardsmen as a whole: active duty, **reserve**, **auxiliary**, and **civilian**.

A coast guard boat patrols New York Harbor near the Statue of Liberty.

THE COAST GUARD'S BEGINNINGS

The first US secretary of the treasury, Alexander Hamilton, didn't want the country to lose money to criminals. The Revenue **Cutter** Service was established in 1790 with 10 ships. It protected the nation's shores from pirates and foreign navies, enforced tax and trade rules, and fought **smuggling**.

As the country grew, expanded its coastlines, and became more involved in international activities, the seagoing service's responsibilities changed. Several departments combined in 1915 to create the US Coast Guard. In 1967, the coast guard came under the management of the Department of Transportation. The newly created Department of Homeland Security took control in 2003.

The Revenue Cutter *Bear* was stationed in Alaska from 1885 to 1926. It was used to stop smugglers and illegal seal hunters, and to help shipwrecked whalers.

Words to Serve By

The coast guard's official motto is *Semper Paratus*, which is Latin for "Always Ready" or "Always Prepared." These words are a good match for the coast guard because it prides itself on being able to respond quickly and effectively to protect US citizens around the world.

HOW THE COAST GUARD IS ORGANIZED

The coast guard is led by the commandant. This four-star admiral, chosen by the president, serves for 4 years and works closely with members of the government and other military branches.

President Barack Obama greets coast guardsmen in Panama City, Florida.

Fast and Flexible

Port security units protect what the coast guard calls assets—piers, harbors, and high-value ships around the world. They may also conduct defense operations alongside other military branches. Mainly staffed by reservists, they can deploy within 96 hours of getting orders and carry enough supplies to support themselves for 30 days.

The coast guard functions in two main areas: the east coast (Atlantic Area) and the west coast (Pacific Area). These areas are broken down into nine districts, which are further broken down into 35 sectors. Sectors may have cutters, aircraft, and deployable units and teams attached to them. Stations located along the nation's coasts work within sectors and use several types of smaller boats for search-and-rescue missions and homeland security duties.

CAREERS IN THE COAST GUARD

As of 2010, the coast guard had over 42,000 active-duty members and close to 8,000 civilian workers. Active-duty members include officers and **enlisted** guardsmen. After 7½ weeks of basic training, newly enlisted members are appointed to a unit for on-the-job training. After gaining experience, they select a **rating** and receive more instruction for their chosen career path.

Coast guard search-and-rescue workers must be ready to jump into action at a moment's notice.

Officers hold leadership positions. Enlisted guardsmen serve as crew members, usually under an officer. A person can become an officer by graduating from the Coast Guard Academy, attending Officer Candidate School, receiving a direct commission, or advancing through the enlisted ranks.

The Coast Guard Academy

The Coast Guard Academy is similar to other colleges. It has academic classes, sports teams, and clubs. Its cadets serve year-round. They spend summers on cutters, training new students, or gaining on-the-job training. After graduating, they must complete at least 5 years of active-duty service.

coast guard recruits during basic training

Some active-duty guardsmen are only part-time members of the coast guard. They often hold nonmilitary jobs. Reservists serve 1 weekend a month and 2 weeks a year. They do the same jobs as regular coast guardsmen and can be called upon to work full-time whenever they're needed. The auxiliary consists of former service members and civilians who volunteer their time to educate **recreational** boaters and watch over seaside communities.

Coast guard cadets aboard the cutter *Eagle* study a chart of the Potomac River.

Many employees of the coast guard are civilians who have no active-duty experience but perform jobs that support coast guard operations. They include lawyers, engineers, and other experts.

Picking a Path

Coast guard ratings are available in the following areas.

- **ship operation: weapons, law enforcement, navigation, communications, intelligence**
- **engineering: electronics, damage control, information systems, machinery**
- **aviation: electric systems, maintenance, survival technology**
- **administration and science: food and health services, marine science, public affairs, storekeeping, human resources**

MISSIONS

The US Coast Guard's 11 official missions fall into three categories. Each coast guardsman, ship, boat, aircraft, and shore station plays an important role in making sure these missions are successful.

Maritime safety means keeping people safe at sea. One of the coast guard's most well-known responsibilities is conducting search-and-rescue operations to save people and property in danger at sea. Search-and-rescue guardsmen use ships and helicopters to rescue people at a moment's notice. Other marine safety duties include looking into accidents, **inspecting** ships, and educating Americans through boating safety programs.

A Challenging Job

Rescue swimmers are dropped or lowered from a helicopter to reach someone in trouble. This could be someone lost at sea, on a cliff, or on a rooftop during a flood. Their training in emergency medical care helps when rescuing sick or injured ship passengers. They can also help maintain and repair aircraft and its equipment.

A search-and-rescue guardsman is lowered from a helicopter during a rescue mission.

Maritime **stewardship** focuses on protecting the environment. The coast guard **enforces** fishing laws, responds to accidents that could harm the ocean, and prevents water pollution. It also makes sure buoys and beacons work properly and keeps waterways free of ice for ships traveling through the area.

On April 21, 2010, coast guard fire boats spray water on the Deepwater Horizon oil rig in the Gulf of Mexico near New Orleans, Louisiana.

Science at Sea

Polar icebreakers don't just clear paths in frozen waterways. They can also serve as seagoing laboratories for both coast guardsmen and civilian scientists. With growing attention on global warming, these coast guard ships will become even more important sources of information about our environment.

Maritime security involves keeping US ports and waterways safe and responding to attacks made on them. It's the coast guard's duty to enforce treaties, agreements, and laws on the sea. Coast guardsmen are trained to keep illegal drugs and migrants from crossing US borders. Maritime security also includes serving with and supporting the US Navy around the world during war and in times of peace.

GETTING THE JOB DONE

The coast guard uses many assets. As of 2010, the coast guard had 250 cutters, 1,784 boats, and 198 aircraft in service. Large cutters can patrol for months at a time, so crews live on the ship. Though usually found in North American and Caribbean waters, they may cross oceans during international missions. Cutters often keep a smaller boat on board for quick, short trips.

America's Tallship

The *Eagle*, built in Germany in 1936, is the only ship in military service that uses traditional sails. It's a barque, or a ship with three or more masts. Cadets use it as a seagoing classroom to practice skills learned in school. Cadets can travel all over the world while assigned to the *Eagle*.

National Security Cutters (NSCs), like the *Waesche* shown here, are the largest cutters in the coast guard. They're 418 feet (127 m) long.

Boats operate close to shore and on inland waterways. They're as small as 12 feet (3.7 m) long and as large as 64 feet (19.5 m) long. Their missions include search and rescue, and port and coastal security.

Coast guardsmen at the Palos Verdes peninsula in California use a helicopter to train for cliff rescues.

Coast guard fixed-wing aircraft (airplanes) perform missions that cover long distances. They're able to carry large loads. Rotary-wing aircraft (helicopters) manage tight turns and direction changes well, and they can take off from and land on the flight decks of larger cutters. In the Caribbean, they're used to stop drug smugglers and illegal immigrants traveling by boat.

The coast guard maintains the **navigation** aids that ship pilots rely on to stay on course and avoid dangers on the water. Examples are lighthouses and lightships, fog signals (bells, whistles, and horns), and buoys.

Four-Legged and Feathered Coasties

From the days when cats controlled a ship's rat population to the K-9 teams used today, animals have long contributed to the coast guard's success. Sometimes pets live on board just to keep the crew members' spirits up. Ship mascots have included dogs, birds, cats, a pig, and even a bear!

DURING WARTIME

In times of war and at the president's request, the coast guard can serve under the Department of Defense. It has taken part in major military actions since the War of 1812. This means working in both US waters—as during the Civil War—and international regions. The coast guard's main roles are to strengthen the navy with men, ships, and aircraft, and to perform missions requiring skills held by coast guardsmen. Jobs include watching for enemy submarines, carrying troops, and rescuing people involved in maritime attacks. Cutters can provide **escorts** to navy ships making long or risky journeys.

Coast guard troops watch as US and Japanese planes battle above them during World War II.

Women in the Coast Guard

Women began serving with the coast guard as lighthouse keepers in the 1830s. These women often performed rescues as well. Their role grew during World War II when they were first hired as civilian employees in the Women's Reserve, or SPARs. Women were first allowed to become active-duty members in 1973.

RESPONDING TO DISASTER

In 2005, the coast guard saved over 33,500 people after Hurricane Katrina. In 2010, the coast guard brought aid to victims of a terrible earthquake in Haiti. Man-made problems—like major oil spills in 1989 and 2010—often require fast responses, too. After a terrorist attack on New York City on September 11, 2001, the coast guard quickly shut down the Port of New York and carried people to safety by water.

The coast guard responds to trouble in other countries, too. During the 1980 Mariel boatlift, more than 125,000 Cubans attempted to make the risky journey to Florida. The coast guard saved many lives that year.

Coast guard cutter *Tohoma* patrols the waters around New York City in the days after the attacks of September 11, 2001.

A coast guard helicopter lifts a person to safety in New Orleans after Hurricane Katrina.

All in a Day's Work

While the coast guard saves an average of 11 people per day, it also performs large-scale rescues. In 1980, the *Prisendam* burned in Alaska's icy waters, but the efforts of helicopter and cutter crews made sure all 520 people on board the ship escaped. In 2007, the service marked 1 million lives saved since 1790.

NOTABLE COAST GUARDSMEN

Coast guardsmen have often been recognized for bravery. Douglas Munro (1919–1942) was awarded the **Medal of Honor** after he died to save a group of marines during World War II. Joshua James (1826–1902) served for 60 years and has been called the world's "most celebrated lifesaver." Richard Etheridge (1842–1900) was the first African American to command a life-saving station. He was known for demanding order and training from the first all–African American crew. This paid off in 1896 when the guardsmen rescued the entire crew of the *E. S. Newman* during a major storm.

Douglas Munro

Douglas Munro is the only coast guardsman ever to receive the Medal of Honor.

Daniel Burbank

Coasties in Space

Commander Bruce Melnick and Captain Daniel Burbank, both pilots and Coast Guard Academy graduates, were the first coast guardsmen to become astronauts. Chosen by NASA to join the program, they trained for several years. Each participated in two missions, spending hundreds of hours in space.

THE FUTURE OF THE COAST GUARD

To meet the nation's needs, the US Coast Guard regularly assesses its ships and designs and builds new assets. It constantly trains guardsmen to respond to threats on US citizens and the environment. The focus on environmental protection and the military's role in the world is growing, and the coast guard takes these issues seriously.

This new 45-foot (13.7 m) response boat patrols the water near New London, Connecticut.

What's in a Name?

All coast guard cutters of the same size share similar names. The new Fast Response Cutters—like the one shown here—are 154 feet (47 m) long. Each of the 58 ships is named for a coast guard hero who, through an act of bravery, saved the lives of others.

The service's core values are "Honor, Respect, and Devotion to Duty." By keeping them in mind as it moves forward, the US Coast Guard can stay true to its beginnings and continue to grow as an important tool for the United States, its citizens, and sailors around the world.

GLOSSARY

auxiliary: referring to civilian volunteers who provide support to a military when needed

civilian: a person not on active duty in the military

cutter: any coast guard ship 65 feet (19.8 m) long or longer

deploy: to move troops into a position of readiness

disaster: an event that causes much suffering or loss

enforce: to make sure people obey the law

enlisted: having to do with a guardsman who is not an officer

escort: a ship or aircraft that accompanies another ship and protects it from attack

inspect: to look over something carefully

maritime: relating to the sea or sailing

Medal of Honor: the highest military honor awarded to US soldiers

navigation: the science of plotting and following a path from one place to another

rating: a general job area in the coast guard that consists of specific skills

recreational: something done for pleasure or relaxation

reserve: referring to soldiers who are not part of a country's main forces, but may be called to active duty in times of need

smuggling: importing or exporting goods illegally

stewardship: the responsibility for environmental quality shared by all those whose actions affect the environment

FOR MORE INFORMATION

Books

David, Jack. *United States Coast Guard.* Minneapolis, MN: Bellwether Media, 2008.

Demarest, Chris L. *Mayday! Mayday! A Coast Guard Rescue.* New York, NY: Margaret K. McElderry Books, 2004.

Goldish, Meish. *Coast Guard: Civilian to Guardian.* New York, NY: Bearport Publishing, 2011.

Websites

Coast Guard Channel
www.coastguardchannel.com
Watch videos of the coast guard in action.

United States Coast Guard
uscg.mil
Read the latest coast guard news and get more information about the service.

US Coast Guard and Coast Guard Reserve
www.gocoastguard.com
Learn about careers in the coast guard.

Publisher's note to educators and parents: Our editors have carefully reviewed these websites to ensure that they are suitable for students. Many websites change frequently, however, and we cannot guarantee that a site's future contents will continue to meet our high standards of quality and educational value. Be advised that students should be closely supervised whenever they access the Internet.

INDEX